YOUR KNOWLEDGE HAS VALUE

- We will publish your bachelor's and master's thesis, essays and papers

- Your own eBook and book - sold worldwide in all relevant shops

- Earn money with each sale

Upload your text at www.GRIN.com and publish for free

Bibliographic information published by the German National Library:

The German National Library lists this publication in the National Bibliography; detailed bibliographic data are available on the Internet at http://dnb.dnb.de .

This book is copyright material and must not be copied, reproduced, transferred, distributed, leased, licensed or publicly performed or used in any way except as specifically permitted in writing by the publishers, as allowed under the terms and conditions under which it was purchased or as strictly permitted by applicable copyright law. Any unauthorized distribution or use of this text may be a direct infringement of the author s and publisher s rights and those responsible may be liable in law accordingly.

Imprint:

Copyright © 2015 GRIN Verlag
Print and binding: Books on Demand GmbH, Norderstedt Germany
ISBN: 9783668724747

This book at GRIN:

https://www.grin.com/document/428789

Jackie Curran

Contemporary Counselling Theories and Techniques and how they relate to a Counsellor's Practice

GRIN Verlag

GRIN - Your knowledge has value

Since its foundation in 1998, GRIN has specialized in publishing academic texts by students, college teachers and other academics as e-book and printed book. The website www.grin.com is an ideal platform for presenting term papers, final papers, scientific essays, dissertations and specialist books.

Visit us on the internet:

http://www.grin.com/

http://www.facebook.com/grincom

http://www.twitter.com/grin_com

A review of contemporary Counselling theories and techniques and how they relate to a Counsellor's Practice

The Importance of Theory in a Counsellor's Practice

All counselling approaches may require a basis in theory, particularly *person-centred counselling* (Davies, 2012) which seems to necessitate a practitioner to have strong theoretical acumen to be successful. There seems to be a large disparity and diversity in individuals who receive counselling, therefore it may be appropriate to retain an applicable knowledge of theory. This knowledge can be selected and applied as and when it is deemed suitable by the counsellor.

Boy and Pine (1990) claim that theory provides a framework, as well as relatedness and unity of information and it allows one to see important client details that may otherwise be overlooked through a more rudimentary approach. Theory may facilitate a logical direction for a developing Counsellor, helping them to focus on relevant information, and provides guidelines for treatment. It is important to know and understand the theory of counselling therapy as it forms the 'skeleton' of counselling practice, with the skills and relationship with clients being the 'meat on the bones.' If the counsellor can understand the theory and the rationale behind it then they can be enact it in their practice. It will aid counsellors to focus and be able to be organised in their thoughts. Theory enables the practitioner to build and sustain a rapport with clients. It also helps to challenge Counsellors to be innovative and compassionate within the professional relationship. It may also act as an evaluation tool for the counsellor to measure their practice and develop professionally. Using the associated skills developed from studying theory, Counsellors are able to integrate different *modalities* into their sessions and can adapt their approach to different situations. This is a valuable tool to use, to tailor the methodology for each individual client in a bespoke and personalised form of therapy (Davies, 2012).

Even if theories are widely accepted, the basis of them can still be challenged. Since Freud, who is widely regarded by some as the father of modern psychology (Schultz and Schultz, 2015) published his landmark theories, eminent researchers such as Carl Rogers, Aaron Beck and Fritz Perls have challenged his work and promulgated alternative approaches.

Person-Centred Theory

Person-Centred Counselling (PCC) was devised by Carl Rogers (1902-1987), also the founder of Humanistic psychology. He believed that clients are the experts in their own life and can help themselves utilising a non-directive approach. Humanistic theories are concerned with the client's freedom, choice and values. Rogers' theory is associated with Maslow's (1970) hierarchy of needs and his theory of human motivation. He used self-actualising as part of the person-centred approach. Like Maslow, Rogers emphasised the importance of *self-actualisation*, the process of growing and developing as a person in order to achieve their ultimate potential.

The Humanistic approach states that knowledge is based on experience of phenomena, what is perceived whilst experiencing any event; therefore everything matters in personal development. Rogers' aim was to provide the optimum climate to become a fully functioning person and he did this through what he termed 'core conditions'.

The first core condition is *congruence*, which means genuineness and according to Rogers is an important attribute of the Counsellor. This is unlike the psychodynamic therapist who generally maintains a 'blank screen' and reveals little of their own personality in therapy.

Secondly, Unconditional Positive Regard (UPR) is accepting a client unconditionally without judging them. The client can then talk freely about their emotions and thoughts in a safe environment. Rogers advocated UPR as being of great importance in the healing process. He suggested that individuals who do not have this type of acceptance from people in their life can eventually come to hold strong, entrenched negative beliefs about themselves. This could lead to low self-esteem and an increased susceptibility to mental illness.

Rogers (1969) concluded that the important elements of empathy are that the therapist understands the client's feelings; the therapist's responses reflects the client's mood and the content of what has been said and the therapist's tone of voice conveys the ability to share the Client's feelings. Finally, it is only when the counsellor is open and sensitive to the emotions and feelings of their client that an authentic relationship can begin. The therapeutic relationship is vital to aid and assist the client to resolve their own issues, to grow as a person and trust their own instincts.

Rogers thought that there were seven stages of progress that could be observed in a client's path to recovery. This helps practitioners to make an assessment of whether clients are making progress in therapy, or whether they seem to be stuck and unable to move on. Although the process can be erratic, clients do in general, progress step by step and sequentially, building on their experiences at one stage before moving on to the next. Only when clients feel accepted and understood at one stage, can they progress to the next one.

Psychodynamic Approaches

The Psychodynamic approach was pioneered by Sigmund Freud (1856-1939) and it is the base of all psychological theory. His theories are clinical as they are derived from therapy with patients. Freud's theories were psychoanalytic; the term 'psychodynamic' refers to both his theories and those of his followers. The Freudian approach was scientific, where the patient is treated and prescripted or directed. His theory assumed that all behaviour has a cause even though it may be unconscious. The Psychodynamic approach states that behaviour and feelings often stem from childhood and are affected by unconscious motives, with all behaviour having a cause/rationale. Freud also used dream analysis to get a theoretical understanding of his patient's subconscious.

He recognised that personalities comprised of three systems, the id, ego and super ego. The id is the unconscious comprising of Eros which is the sex drive and life instincts and Thanatos which is an aggressive drive and death instinct. It does not have a sense of right or wrong, is impulsive and is irrational. It comprises of the most basic of human instincts and drives. He believed that the unconscious mind was engaged in a constant battle with the conscious mind or ego. The ego is the site of the reality principle; it is realistic and logical and is continuously checking the impulsive nature of the id (Freud, 1923).

The superego sets the ideal moral code for the individual. It operates on the moral principle which rewards the individual for following traditional values and what is expected in society. When a person violates the ideal ego denying or ignoring the rules of the superego then the person feels guilt. The personality is then changed by the conflicts of the above components throughout childhood. Freud thought that the first few years of our lives were crucial to our future development. The relationships we establish, the way we are treated by our parents and many of our other experiences have a huge impact to the structure of our psyche and the personality and behaviour we display as adults. Freud (1920) believed that childhood development went in stages. At each stage, different parts of the psyche are developed and different influences become important. The stages go in a fixed order and a relatively fixed time scale. Problems in adulthood can usually be traced back to issues that first arose during a particular stage of development.

Psychodynamic therapies centre on revealing and resolving the conflicts that are driving their symptoms. The goals help to bring an unresolved developmental conflict or repressed trauma into the conscious from the unconscious, in turn this gives insight and self- awareness.

Cognitive Behavioural Therapy (CBT) was formulated by Aaron Temkin Beck, an American psychiatrist with a particular interest in neurology.

Beck (1967) logically deduced that there is a positive correlation between the amount and severity of someone's negative thoughts about themselves and their environment and the severity of their depressive symptoms. The more negative thoughts that are experienced, the more depressed the person becomes. According to Beck, a depressed person sees their past, present and future from an entirely negative viewpoint. The depressed person will feel inadequate, with all experiences being failures and the future seeming hopeless. These three themes are described as the *Negative Cognitive Triad*. When these beliefs are present in someone's cognition, depression is very likely to occur. The aim is to help the person feel safe to challenge their assumptions, look at their fears and change their behaviour. This might include helping people to gradually face feared or avoided situations as a means to reducing anxiety and learning new behavioural skills to tackle problems.

CBT addresses three important factors; cognition (a way of thinking), emotion (a way of feeling) and behaviour (a way of acting). The cognitive elements of this theory refer to how people think about and understand situations, symptoms and events in their lives and how beliefs are developed about themselves, others and the world. Cognitive therapy uses techniques to help people become more aware of how they think. The behaviour element refers to the way people respond when they are upset and distressed. Typical responses can include trying to use avoidance tactics so that they are not dealing the problem. The person can exhibit unhelpful behaviour which can exacerbate the stress of situations.

CBT can help make sense of problems by breaking them down into smaller constituent parts. This makes it easier to see how they are all interconnected and how they affect the person. CBT looks at a situation and compartmentalises it into thoughts, emotions, physical feelings and actions. The aim is to help the person feel safe to challenge their assumptions, look at their fears and modify their behavior accordingly. To get the desired results, this therapy is normally used in conjunction with medication and can help with numerous disorders, particularly depression. It is an evidence-based theory, Clinical trials have proven its effectiveness and it has been adapted and accepted all over the world (Butler and Beck, 2000).

A criticism of many theories is that they present partial truths as whole truths. For instance, Rogers theorises a universal diagnosis of all clients' problems, namely that there is incongruence between self-structure and experience and sees relationship conditions as necessary in all instances (Rogers, 1951). Freud emphasises uncovering unconscious material through the analysis of dreams, but says little about developing specific effective behaviours to deal with everyday problems. The trend to use a variety of modalities where therapists draw upon aspects from different theories, attests to this negative aspect of some major theories.

Supervision

According to the British Association of Counselling and Psychotherapy (BACP), the nature of clinical supervision is an intervention provided by a more senior member of a profession to a more junior member of that same profession. Supervision is important in supporting the practitioner to stick to the ethical framework and is essential to monitor and review the quality of work, as well as reviewing a client's progress. Clinical Supervision exists for two reasons, to protect the Client and to improve the ability of Counsellors to provide value to their clients. In the UK, the (BACP) requires all accredited Therapists to have supervision throughout their career.

Supervision is a professional service for counsellors. Dawson (2013) describes supervision as a formal arrangement and it can be on a one to one basis, it may be as part of a group or selection of peers and occasionally it may be in the room during a counselling session. As it is formal arrangement, it is necessary to have a contract with a supervisor. Included in the contract will be confidentiality although this may need to be breached if a client discloses harm to themselves, a child or another person. It will contain details of the fees, the venue details, time and frequency of supervision sessions.

Dawson (2013) states that all counsellors benefit from having regular professional supervision. A supervisor acts in a mentoring role as a consultant to the counsellor, providing emotional and pastoral support as well as information and guidance. It may be needed to help resolve issues and to avoid burnout as self care is very important and is also part of the ethical framework. As well as providing a sounding board for concerns, a supervisor is in a good position to spot any symptoms of burnout and will help the counsellor to deal with this.

Waskett (2006) furthers elaborates on the positives of supervision: counsellors can develop a sense of professional identity and be able to examine beliefs and attitude regarding Clients and therapy. A Supervisor can challenge the practitioner to make sure that they working ethically, developing and broaden their knowledge in the process.

Discussing counselling sessions with a supervisor and getting feedback will help a Counsellor to gain an objective insight into their own performance and skills. It provides an opportunity to learn and practice new skills and to find better ways to help clients. It is common among practitioners that they can encounter obstacles in a particular situation with a client, their client disengages and sometimes little progress is made. This reluctance may come from client's need for self-protection but can often lead to therapeutic breakthroughs. Supervision can play an especially important role in helping practitioners to address these moments. Good supervision is not about therapy for the counsellor, but a focus on ways in which the counsellor impacts on the client, the therapeutic relationship, the supervisor and the supervisory relationship.

Conclusion

In PCC, the Counsellor understands the client by developing a professional relationship with them. The use of Rogers' theory as a framework and the Counsellor's personal qualities should help to build the therapeutic relationship with the client. Person-Centred Counsellors tend to have a very positive outlook, potentially making it a more beneficial therapy for clients.

Conversely, a psychodynamic approach can also be advantageous as it enables the client to experience and accept more of who they are, reconnecting with their own values and sense of self-worth. This reconnection with their inner resources enables them to find their own way to move forward, with the help of CBT to allow them to think more optimistically about life.

Good supervision is also essential, as it allows for honest assessment of a counsellor and their practice and the manner in which they impact upon the client, the therapeutic relationship, the supervisor and the supervisory relationship. This allows the counsellor to observe the Client's experience from the Client's point of view.

Ultimately, there does seem to be a growing trend for different approaches of counselling to be informed by theory and research, as evidenced by the popularity of CBT. If these theories are coupled with sound supervision, this could result in a very effective style of counselling for clients.

References

Beck, A. T. (1967) *Depression: Causes and treatment.* Philadelphia: University of Pennsylvania Press.

Boy, A.V. and Pine, G. (1990) *A Person-Centered Foundation for Counseling and Psychotherapy.* Springfield, Illinois: Charles C. Thomas Publisher.

Butler, A. C. and Beck, J. S. (2000) 'Cognitive therapy outcomes: A review of meta-analyses.', *Journal of the Norwegian Psychological Association*, 37, 1-9.

Davies, N. (2012) *Theories of Counselling: Why are they important?* [Online]. Available at: http://healthpsychologyconsultancy.wordpress.com/2012/10/01/theories-of-counselling-why-are-they-important/ (Accessed: 25 May 2015).

Dawson, R. (2013) *Counselling/clinical supervision* [Online].

Available at:

http://www.counsellingpsychologist.com/supervision.htm (Accessed: 20 June 2015).

Freud, S. (1920) *Beyond the pleasure principle.* SE, 18: 1-64.

Freud, S. (1923) *The ego and the id.* SE, 19: 1-66.

Maslow, A. H. (1970) *Motivation and personality.* New York: Harper & Row.

McLeod, S. A. (2008) *Psychosexual Stages - Simply Psychology.* [Online].

Available at:

http://www.simplypsychology.org/psychosexual.html_(Accessed: 16 June 2015).

Rogers, C. (1951) *Client-centered Therapy: Its Current Practice, Implications and Theory.* London: Constable.

Rogers, C. (1969) 'A theory of therapy, personality, and interpersonal relationships, as developed in the client-centred framework'. *Psychology: A Study of a Science*, 3. New York: Penguin.

Schultz, D. P. and Schultz, S. E. (2015) *A History of Modern Psychology.* Boston, MA: Cengage Learning.

Waskett, C. (2006) 'The pluses of solution-focused supervision', *Healthcare Counselling and Psychotherapy Journal*, 6, (1).

YOUR KNOWLEDGE HAS VALUE

- We will publish your bachelor's and master's thesis, essays and papers

- Your own eBook and book - sold worldwide in all relevant shops

- Earn money with each sale

Upload your text at www.GRIN.com and publish for free